# LIFE FOR REAL DUMMIES

"Life for the Totally Clueless"

A Parody
Richard Sandomir & Rick Wolff

HarperPerennial
*A Division of* HarperCollins*Publishers*

HarperCollins books may be purchased for educational, business, or sales promotional use.
For information please write: Special Markets Department, HarperCollins Publishers, Inc.,
10 East 53rd Street, New York, NY 10022.

"...FOR DUMMIES" and all related marks, logos, characters, designs, and trade dress
are trademarks under exclusive license to IDG Books Worldwide, Inc., from
International Data Group, Inc.

FIRST EDITION

*Designed by Marlitt Dellabough*

*Illustrations by Matt Maley*

*Produced by Connor & Downey*

ISBN 0-06-095207-5

96 97 98 99 00 ◊/RRD 10 9 8 7 6 5 4 3 2 1

# Acknowledgments

The authors owe a great debt to the following, without whom **Life for Real Dummies** would not have been possible:

Our wives, Griffin Miller and Patty Wolff, who know how dumb we really are; our parents, who look at us and shake their heads; Mauro DiPreta, our editor, who rewards witlessness handsomely, as does his assistant, Kristen Auclair; Jack Rapoport, Esq., of the law firm Dewey, Cheatem & Howe; Tom Connor and Jim Downey, our inane packagers; Rob McMahon, who endures Rick's duncery daily; Arlen Schumer, who can take insipid concepts and turn them into idiotic illustrations; Steve Urkel, to whom we pray nightly; Vinny Holland, our photographic consultant, who invented the one-shot camera for dummies; Al Bundy, who inspires us every day; Rachel McClain, who took an existing cover concept and copied it shamelessly; the writers of the "Grumpy Old Man" films, whose words greatly enhanced our SEX FOR REAL DUMMIES chapter; Biscuit Griffin, a cat so sublime that other cats resent her; Morris, Sam and Jerry Horowitz plus Larry Fineberg, Stooges four; and IDG Books Worldwide, which publishes the "DUMMIES" series and would be dumb if it did not laugh at the knuckleheaded homage we've given their creation.

## About the Authors

Richard Sandomir wore a toupee for six weeks in 1990. By day, he is the TV sports columnist for The New York Times. Really.

Rick Wolff keeps an extra set of keys in his glove compartment in case he locks himself out of his car. In real life, he is a senior editor at Warner Books.

# INTRODUCTION: HOW TO USE THIS BOOK...

*"We used to be dumb—really dumb—just like you. But now we're just* plain *dumb, and we feel compelled to pass our wisdom on to you."*

—Richard Sandomir and Rick Wolff

If nothing else, **Life for Real Dummies** is truly that—a vital handbook of not just how to survive, but how to actually thrive in life.

Forget what you've read about life being "full of mysteries" and "like a box of chocolates." The truth is, life is unbelievably predictable—all the way from infancy to childhood to adulthood and into old age. Except for the occasional mutant adaptation, with mankind being what it is today, what you see is pretty much what you get.

To that end, **Life for Real Dummies** has been especially written and designed for the lowest common denominator of *homo sapiens*—i.e., you. (In other words, if you can't follow the directions here, you're in deep trouble.) And to that end, here's a quick rundown of how to use this book for maximum impact:

**1. Hold the Book in Your Hands.** For those of you who aren't experienced in reading a book, you'll find that it's infinitely easier to hold the book in such a position so the printing on the cover and inside pages are readable.

If you have difficulty in comprehending the material on the printed page, chances are you're holding the book upside down.

**2. Turn to the Table of Contents.** On this page, which is located on one of the first few pages of the book, you'll find a complete listing of all of the essential topics in life.

Not only will you find each section of the book listed, but you'll also find a corresponding page number to each listed section. If you want to turn to a particular section, you merely have to turn to the page number that's listed next to it in the **Table of Contents.**

**3. Page Numbers.** For your convenience, you'll discover that the pages in **Life for Dummies** are conveniently numbered—in numerical order. The book starts on page 1 and continues, in order, right up to the end of the book.

**4. After You Finish Reading a Page, turn to the Next One.** Take the page on the right and turn it to the left. You should be facing a brand-new page of text. (Note: If you turn the page the other way, chances are you'll be reading a page that you have read only moments before.)

To double-check yourself, make a mental note of what page you started on, then see what page you're on now. In other words, if you started on page 34, when you complete that page you should find yourself starting to read page 35. And so on.

**5. Glossary.** For your reading convenience, there's a glossary located at the end of the book. Be sure to use it!

# THE CAST OF ICONS

 **Tip** Try this. If you're dumb enough.

 **Help Me!** Beware of guidance purposely written to be wrong and which could permanently disembowel you.

 **Go Slow** Go slow.

 **BS Warning** Stop and smell that poop! If you follow this, you may get in trouble with the IRS, the IRA, the FBI, the SEC, the NCAA, IBM, the BBC, MDA, the CIA, the F.A.L.N., MTV, and U.N.C.L.E.

 **Look Out!** This will be a task as difficult as telling a cumulus nimbus cloud from a romulus imus formation.

 **Remember This!** Don't forget. Forgetting is not remembering what you knew. We forgot why a string tied to your middle finger means remember.

 **Out of Gas–Push** So simple even a putz would understand this.

 **CrossReference** Indicates where information on the same subject can be found in lesser depth in another publication.

 **Apocalypse** You're doomed.

# Contents

# Chapter 1

# SEX FOR REAL DUMMIES

From an historical perspective, nobody really knows for certain when sex was invented. Leading social anthropologists have studied this evolutionary process for many years, and so far their best guess was that the sexual act (or sex, as we call it today) probably started around 12,000 years ago.

Before then, most members of the *homo sapien* species tended to be short, stooped creatures with fur all over their bodies. Even by today's lowly regarded mating standards, the male or female of the species from 12,000 years ago was not exactly the most desirable individual. But human nature being as indomitable as it is, a few rounds of fermented hops, dim campfire light, and—voilà—sex was invented.

Where did sex begin? There is some scientific evidence that sex started in central Europe. Most of the earliest records of these sexually active people indicate that they spoke with a thick Germanic accent, tended to be short (under five feet tall), and compulsively acted as if they knew everything about sex. (Some of their descendants are still around today in the form of popular guests on talk shows.)

# How Sex Has Evolved Through Time

Just like so many other genetic and social aspects of humankind, the sexual act has also evolved dramatically over the years. Indeed, there have been all sorts of waves of differing sexual practices, not only in terms of different tribes and societies, but also in the physical act of love-making itself.

- It is theorized by paleoanthropologists that Neanderthals had sex in a matter of mere minutes. The male would engage in minimal foreplay with his female partner before mounting her and consummating the sexual act.

- Sex also had a distinctive pattern in hunter-gatherer nomadic tribes. Because of the fear of being attacked by warring tribes, sex was consummated relatively quickly. The male would engage in minimal foreplay with his female partner before mounting her and consummating the sexual act.

- In Greek and Roman times sexual promiscuity was rampant. Both men and women couldn't wait to jump from one partner to the next. To accommodate these libidinal urges, the male would have minimal foreplay with his female partner before mounting her and consummating the sexual act.

- In the Middle Ages sexual promiscuity was also quite common, but due to the constant difficulty encountered with chastity belts and suits of armor, the male would have minimal foreplay with his female partner before quickly mounting her and consummating the sexual act.

- In Victorian times sex was hardly ever discussed openly. As such, it was preferred that the male would have minimal foreplay with his female partner before quickly mounting her and consummating the sexual act.

- In the 1960s "free love" was all the rage with hippies (now baby boomers). To spread the message of love, sexual partners would be exchanged constantly. To do that, the male would have minimal foreplay with his female partner before quickly mounting her and consummating the sexual act.

- It's predicted that by year 2000, sexual habits will have come full circle from the earliest days of male/female encounters—from the Golden Age of Greece to the hippie days of free love. As a result, social experts predict that the male will have minimal foreplay with the female partner...

## *Determining Your Sex*

The first thing you have to determine is what sex you are. Today, you have a choice. Male. Female. Bisexual. Trisexual.

Rather than go into a confusing discourse about the biological differences among these different sexes, here's a quick way for you to figure out your sexual identity:

If you find yourself breathing heavily, your eyes transfixed on bikini-clad women, and notice all sorts of physiological changes taking place in your body, then chances are you are MALE.

If you find yourself wistfully daydreaming, your eyes transfixed on hunky guys, and notice all sorts of physiological changes taking place in your body, then chances are you are FEMALE.

If you find yourself attracted to common, garden-variety earthworms, which are born with both male and female sexual organs, then chances are you are BISEXUAL.

If you find yourself attracted to tricycles, then chances are you are TRISEXUAL.

## *How the Various Parts Fit Together*

Occasionally, the sexual act can become a bit of a tight squeeze if the body parts from male and female don't match up. As most sexually active people know, this is a common problem. (Some people have commented that the sexual act is sometimes like trying to stuff a square peg in a round hole. Well, that's where lubricants come into play—keep reading).

Fortunately, there are a number of routine household remedies available. Traditionally, K-Y lubricating jelly and Vaseline petroleum jelly (which are both normally used for throwing a nasty spitter), can also be applied to the male sexual organ as a lubricant. In addition, you can use shaving cream, toothpaste, Pam, orange Jell-o, glovolium, 3-in-1 oil, and pine tar. And if you're in a car away from home, a quick dash of Havoline 10-40 motor oil can also do the trick, but one caution: It does tend to leave a stain.

## *How to Recognize When He Wants to Have Sex with You*

If you have ever spent much time in a singles' bar, you know firsthand how confusing sexual overtures can be. People on the prowl don't normally come up to you and say, "Hello, can I have sex with you?"

Unfortunately, it's not that simple or direct. As a result, a great deal of confusion can occur, particularly when two people of the opposite sex are trying to reach a mutual consensus about a mutual act. To help you plow through this maze of confusion, here's a quick guide to help you understand what he's saying and what he really means.

# *What He Says...and What He Means*

* "How 'bout I take my skinboat to tuna town..."

  This is an old colloquial expression from New England whaling days, meaning that the gentleman would love to take you away on a long, sunny cruise to the Caribbean, where tuna and other large slippery fish run wild.

* "How 'bout I put my hot dog in your bun?"

  An expression from the sports world. It means that it's so crowded that perhaps you might want to sit on his lap and see what pops up during conversation.

* "How 'bout a ride on the wild baloney pony?"

  He wants to know if you want to go out on a date with him to the local amusement park and check out the latest rides. Caution: He'll probably take you on a ride that calls for a lot of casual contact.

* "How 'bout I take the old log to the beaver?"

  He wants to know if you would like to go on a walk in the woods and commune, together, with him, animals, and nature.

* "How 'bout I slip you the old salami?"

  Just another way of him asking you whether he can buy you lunch or dinner. Be certain to say "yes" enthusiastically.

# *Safe Sex: Does It Exist?*

There is no such thing as safe sex. Every kind of sexual activity involves some sort of risk. That's just the way it is.

Here's a complete chart, with the actual risk percentages shown, of contacting a sexually transmitted disease.

| | |
|---|---|
| Having sex with someone you don't know | 5% |
| Having sex on the Internet | 14% |
| Having sex with yourself | 11% |
| Having sex with your cousin | 10% |
| Having sex with a sheep | 89% |
| Having sex with an inflatable doll | 45% |
| Having sex with Madonna | 0% |
| Having sex with Michael Jackson* | |

*Doesn't have sex, so this can't be calculated.*

## How Often Are You Having Sex?

 The vast majority of red-blooded Americans worry constantly about how much sex they're having, and whether their friends and neighbors are having more than they are.

## Quiz: How often do Americans have sex?

— College-educated, household income over $50,000: at least eighteen times a week, which includes twelve sexual encounters with colleagues at work, three with nannies/babysitters, two with neighbors, one with spouse on Saturday night.

— UPS and FedEx drivers: Ever notice how happy UPS and FedEx delivery men are? Well, they score hourly, per stop.

 — Your parents: Among the most sexually active. Good thing menopause exists, or else Florida would be going through another baby boom and Grandma would be sharing her Depends with her newborn.

## Chapter 2

# WINDOWS 96 FOR REAL DUMMIES

What was all that fuss about Windows 95? A window is a window, even if you get all hifalutin and capitalize the *W*. You open a window, you close a window, you clean a window. You can't improve on a classic. Do you see anyone coming out with Wheels 96? Of course not. A wheel is a wheel. Even if you capitalize the *W*.

## *Getting to Know Windows 96*

If you're an old hand at raising, lowering, and breaking windows, then you may not need Windows 96. But stick around. You might learn something about the nuances of opening a window with a crank. Windows 96 has added a further understanding of bay windows.

## *Understanding Windows 96*

Put very, very simply, a WINDOW can be a little box, a medium box, or a really, really big box that you see through because it's made of glass, which is generally a transparent material.

- You can see a WINDOW with the naked eye.

- You can see a WINDOW through a piece of plastic called a contact lens that is placed over your eye.

- You can see a WINDOW through little framed windows perched on your nose, which are called glasses.

If you look through a WINDOW too close to the WINDOW, the WINDOW will fog up. Do not be alarmed. This is a natural occurrence called CONDENSATION. You are not in the early stages of glaucoma.

**Cross-Reference:** See *Air for Dummies*.

## *Using a Mouse to Open a Window*

This is why you're a Real Dummy. Only a mouse injected with enough cyclamates to cause cancer in a human being could open a window on its own.

## *How Do I Get to Windows?*

To access a window, walk to almost any part of a house or building where light is coming through glass. If you drive down any number of streets in the world, you will see that almost every building has a window.

## *Parts of a Window*

Components used to maximize, for example, your use of a double-hung Windows 96 include:

| Window Part | Function |
| --- | --- |
| Pane | Individual part or parts of a window that lets you see what's on the other side and control all applications. |
| Sill | Bottom of window. Where dirt and dead bugs collect. |
| Lock | Lock out unwanted users. |
| Sash | Parts of window frame that go up and down with push of scroll buttons. |

## *To Open Windows*

The control menu attached to every window is a short list of commands that are especially useful to all people who crave air circulation in their home or office. Just push the command you need for the window task you require.

## *To Close Windows*

## *Controlling Your Windowpane*

The windowpane is the heart of your window. Without a pane, big or small, minimized or maximized or even dragged across the room by a mouse, your window is absolutely useless. Once you find the pane you can work wonders with its many applications. When you select your control windowpane, you see the following:

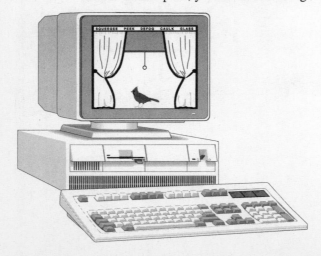

# *Accessories for Windows 96*

There are many available accessories. Venetian blinds, miniblinds, microblinds, minimicroblinds, blinds that go vertical, blinds that go horizontal. Valances. Sashes. Curtains. Drapes. Bars and gates. Strings that open and close blinds.

***To open the curtain accessory to Windows 96, follow these steps:***
1. Find the string.

2. Click on the string. For good luck.

3. Pull the string toward you. No one knows at first if that will open or close the curtain. Pull it. See what happens.

***To open the blinds accessory, follow these steps:***
1. Find the pole.

2. Twist the pole one way or the other. The blinds may open, they may close.

3. To clean blinds, call the 800-WINDOWS 96 housekeeper service.

# *Doing Everyday Junk in Windows 96*

### *Arranging Icons in a Window*

Take the wayward icons you've had sitting idle in drawers and decorate your windows with stick-on decals of Jesus, Elvis, Abe Lincoln, Buddha, Clint Eastwood, Santa Claus, Deion Sanders, Joe Namath, Wayne Gretzky, or Wynonna Judd.

### *How Do I Do It?*

Don't line them up willy-nilly on any old window in your house. Make a diagram on a piece of paper. Arrange them on your bed in a nice design. Then peel off the backings and stick them neatly on the window.

### *Changing the View Options for a Window*

- If you're sitting down, stand up.

- If you're on the left side of the window, move to the right.

- Close one eye. Then close the other.

- Move to the back of the room. Then return to the front.

- Lay down on the bed.

- Sit on the sill.

If you want to sharpen the view, bash the window with a hammer.

## *Using Remote Control to Move Car Windows*

Those who remember the manual controls for cars in WINDOWS 3.1 may need a little brush-up on remote window control. In such an advanced WINDOWS 96 car, the driver has electronic control of all four windows. The person manning any of the other three windows only has control of that individual window. So, the driver can cause your toupee to fly off by surreptitiously opening your window to gusts of wind, but you can create little havoc for him. Depending upon your position, life can suck in Windows 96.

# Chapter 3

# GOLF FOR REAL DUMMIES

## The Attraction of the Game

Nobody is really quite sure why golf has become so popular in recent years. Nor can anyone seem to explain its distinctive addictive quality. After all, most people who play golf come away from a day on the links with nothing more than sheer frustration, heavy drinking bills, and severe debt from lost wages.

Perhaps that's precisely why golf IS so popular: It imitates life in so many ways.

Regardless, it's clear that golf is *the* game in the 1990s, with its own channel on cable television and players bidding up to six figures to belong to famous country clubs.

So what's the big deal about hitting a little pimply ball into a tin cup? Common sense does draw some basic conclusions about the game.

A round of golf on a pleasant day provides the player a chance to mix business with pleasure, to take in some lovely sight-seeing and, of course, to enjoy a fully rigorous and aerobic workout that cleanses both the body and mind.

| Calories Burned from Various Activities* | |
| --- | --- |
| Bowling | 18 calories |
| Sailing | 29 calories |
| Jogging | 80 calories |
| Softball | 170 calories |
| Handball | 400 calories |
| Golf | 1,880 calories |

*(*Assumes a 45-year-old white male, approximately 30 pounds overweight, having full use of a golf cart for 18 holes, a stopover break for several cocktails after the first nine holes, and a long break for more refreshments at the 19th hole.)*

## Getting Dressed for Golf

One of the best aspects of playing golf is that you can wear just about anything you want on the golf course without being embarrassed. Indeed, most of the top pros on the PGA Tour wear outfits that they most likely dug out of a heap of old clothes from the back of their closets.

And for good reason: Top golfers recognize that a day on the links might involve stepping in mud, getting sprayed by some flying divots, or even heading into the bramble brush to retrieve a lost ball or two. As a result, they know that it makes a lot of sense to wear clothing that is comfortable as well as disposable. These include baggy knickers, ugly Ban-Lon shirts, and bizarre pants. In fact, when you think about it, there really is no other place on earth where you could wear such outfits without getting viciously beaten.

This sartorial background should help explain why the most coveted prize in the world of golf happens to be a single piece of clothing—a green jacket. True, it's an awful shade of green, and it rarely fits properly, but that's not the point. Winning the Masters and getting that green jacket is what golf is truly all about: *the chance to wear extremely ugly clothes in public.*

# *The Rules Explained*

Basically, golf is a very simple game. Whoever gets the ball into the 18 little holes with the fewest number of strokes wins. True, there are some rules thrown in during the course of play. But in general, these so-called formal rules of play only get in the way of your enjoyment and can be easily overlooked.

### Tip #1: The rules of the game
If one of your playing partners does happen to protest that you're breaking one of the sacred rules of the game, just feign ignorance and make a stern face at your colleague, as if to say, "What are you trying to do, ruin my fun?"

### Tip #2: How to address the ball
In the world of golf, Edward Norton, author of *If You Play Golf Then You're an Idiot*, popularized the common practice of addressing the ball by first tipping your hat to your ball and saying hello to it.

### Tip #3: Your golf glove
Always be certain to wear a golf glove when playing. Be certain to get a pair that fits.

### Tip #4: A mulligan
A *mulligan* occurs when you hit a lousy tee shot. Feel free to take this shot again and again; it's one of the common courtesies of this very genteel game. Don't worry—nobody will say a thing. If they do, refer to Tip # 1.

# Uncommonly Good Ploys to Insure Victory

Golf, as mentioned above, is a very frustrating game, particularly if you're not very good at it. Here, then, are some guaranteed tips on how to improve your score quickly and painlessly.

**Tip #1:** Smoosh your opponent's ball into the sand trap—one of the better ways to distract his concentration. If he hits his ball into a sand trap, just make certain you get to the trap first, and then—*accidentally*—step on his ball and push it into the sand even further.

**Tip #2:** Keep an extra ball in your pants cuff—an effective strategy whenever you discover your drive has landed in the rough. Just always have the same brand of ball in your baggy pants cuff, and then very discreetly dump that ball into a better lie. Remember: Unless your opponent catches you, it's not really cheating.

**Tip #3:** Put some Vaseline petroleum jelly on your opponent's club handles, put a little slippery elm on his hitting stick, and look out! Great fun for all involved.

**Tip #4:** Electronic pager goes off when your opponent putts. Don't you hate it when someone's beeper goes off while you're playing? Imagine how your opponent will feel when he's trying to sink that six-foot putt and *your* beeper *accidentally* goes off.

**Tip #5:** Reflecting mirror sunglasses in your opponent's face. "Oh, I'm sorry, did the glare from my sunglasses get in your face while you were putting? What a shame..."

**Tip #6:** The flag pull-and-plant strategy. When your opponent is putting, remove the pin from the cup and place your foot over the hole. Let him play out his putt thinking he's really aiming for the cup.

# Getting to Know the PGA: A Fan's Guide

Everybody knows what Jack Nicklaus looks like. Same with Arnold Palmer or Sam Snead. But in today's fast-paced, lookalike world of top golfers, even the most experienced fan needs a little help in identifying the top players. Here's a quick guide:

| Corey Pavin | Davis Love III | Ernie Els | John Daly |

# Golf Etiquette

When playing with women, be polite. Always offer women golfers lots of tips, from Ben Wright's new book, *Golf in the Animal Kingdom: Hitting Them Straight with Big-Teated Cows.*

# How to Play Golf with Your Boss

Easy. Everything for him is a gimme.

# Chapter 4

# COMMUNICATING FOR REAL DUMMIES

. . . . . . . . . . . . . . . . . . . . . . . . . . . . . . . . . . . . . . .

*In this chapter*
- ▶ Learning to shut your mouth
- ▶ Talking to yourself
- ▶ Walking and talking simultaneously

. . . . . . . . . . . . . . . . . . . . . . . . . . . . . . . . . . . . . . .

There's no question that with all the amazing advances in modern technology over the last twenty years, computers have changed the way we interact one another. With all the breakthroughs in e-mail, the Internet, and telephone gadgets like call waiting, call forwarding, caller I.D., and speed dialing, it's becoming difficult to keep up with simple inter-personal communications and intrapersonal contact, such as when two people meet face-to-face and want to express ideas to each other in a continuing manner.

## *Talking: Starting a Chat Session*

In the presence of one or more persons, open your mouth and let WORDS emerge, one after another, in a form commonly known as a sentence. If the other person does not walk away, it is a good sign that you can continue the CHAT.

A CHAT session initiated when nobody else plans to return CHAT to you is considered risky on subways, inside bath-room stalls, and behind post office cashier desks.

Opening your mouth all the way in order to CHAT is not necessary. You may open your mouth halfway. If you're talented enough, you can keep your mouth closed and speak, which is called VENTRILOQUISM. Edgar Bergen was a renowned ventriloquist on the radio who moved his lips. He liked to CHAT with his DUMMY, Charlie McCarthy.

Do not be alarmed to see that various words require your lips to position themselves into different shapes. It is normal, unless your lips contort into balloon zebras.

## Continuing a Chat Session

Sometimes a productive CHAT session includes stopping your mouth and watching the other person's mouth emit sounds and occasional words.

HEARING is considered a positive physical skill, but LISTENING is considered even more important. LISTENING requires that you comprehend the CHAT from the other person and that your words might reflect something to do with his.

## Ending a Chat Session

Stop talking.

Either person can end the CHAT session. To end it, close your mouth and stop thinking of words to say. Then walk in the opposite direction from where the person you were chatting with is standing.

# No More Chat: When You Don't Want to Talk

If you don't want to talk anymore but the other person does:

- Turn your face away

- Walk away

- Flatulate

If you are a famous person trying to disengage from CHAT, the above advice will not work when you are being chased by paparazzi.

If others try to talk to you while you are refusing to talk, inform them that you have ended our CHAT session and would like some quiet.

If others are conducting a CHAT session behind you during a movie, give them dirty looks. If necessary, pelt them with buttered popcorn (the healthier, air-popped variety is too light to cause pain).

If while giving them dirty looks or pelting them with popcorn you notice they are bigger and younger than you, cease all activity, gather your belongings, and move. Their CHAT session is far more important than potential bodily harm to you.

# The Telephone: How to Make It Work for You

Invented by Alexander Graham Bell, the telephone is an instrument that exists to force a CHAT session upon unsuspecting others in possession of another phone.

### Starting a Call

Lift the receiver. Place the end with the littler holes next to your ear. The other end will naturally move next to your mouth.

If you don't hear a dial tone, ringing, or another person's voice, you may have placed the wrong end to your ear. Switch ends. If you still hear nothing, it is appropriate to pay your bill.

**Dialing:** This can be the toughest part of all if you are illiterate, dyslexic, or aren't good with numbers. In the 1960s Barney Fife used to be able to ask Sarah to connect him to anybody he wanted in Mayberry. But modern America is a very different place. Sarah was laid off by AT&T and her 401(k) account was ravaged. She is now homeless. And you must employ your own wits to dial phone numbers by yourself—unless you have a manservant to do it for you.

**The Rotary Way:** The rotary phone is a relic of a bygone age, yet many people's parents still have them. On this phone, you will notice a dial with ten holes in it. Now, looking at the number you want to dial, stick your finger into the matching hole. Ignore the dirt or toejam that builds up inside the holes. James Earl Jones calls it "communications ick," and makes it sound as good as Neo-Synephrine. For each number, push the dial clockwise, which means to the right.

**Pushing Buttons:** Just push the matching button for each number you want. This is better because you can dial faster to call in for radio station prizes or to make an estimated five times more crank calls per hour than you could on a rotary phone.

Be patient. Dial one number at a time.

**Danger Spot:** The area code! They are three digits long. You often have to dial those numbers before you dial the ones you really want. If you want to call Los Angeles from anywhere but Los Angeles, you must dial 213 first. Or 818. Or 310. It depends on where in Los Angeles you want to call. If you had O. J. Simpson's Brentwood phone number, you'd have to dial 310.

**Tip:** There can be many digits in a phone number. A local number will have seven. A long-distance number has 11, including the 1 plus the area code and seven-digit phone number. Many international numbers have as many as 73 individual digits assigned to them.

### Continuing the Call

Proceed by responding to the person talking on the other end. Sometimes you will be asked questions. It is appropriate to answer. You may also ask a question and reasonably expect an answer. The other person may want to swap nasty stories about other people. This is commonly called GOSSIP. This particular type of friendly conversation can last anywhere from a few minutes to many hours.

When the GOSSIP turns to you, then it is called a SCURRILOUS RUMOR.

**Tip:** Teenagers are frequently the primary telephone users in a family. They can be identified as the people in a house with zits so filled with pus that when popped they can shatter unsuspecting mirrors. Do not give these people their own telephone line! Have only one phone and make a point of sitting in the room while they talk. Time their calls with a three-minute egg timer. This will cut their conversation time, cause them to run away, and give you more time to gossip.

### Ending a Call
**Say Good-bye:** No one really knows what good-bye literally means, anymore than why people say HELLO when they pick up the phone. But it is common practice to use hello and good-bye to start and end a conversation. Do not say hello in the middle of a conversation because both people will have to go back to the start of the call. Do not say good-bye in the middle of a phone CHAT because you will most likely hear a click then a dial tone. Then you must re-dial. (For dialing instructions, go back to the beginning of this section.)

When you place the receiver into the CRADLE of the telephone, it is called HANGING UP.

### Ending a Call Without Saying Good-bye
Sometimes you're talking to an in-law or a telemarketer, and you don't want to continue the conversation. You've said enough. You want to go. You're late. You want to go to the bathroom.

**You Don't Have to Keep Talking:** The Telephone Commission permits you to lay the receiver down without the traditional good-bye.

Should a conversation not progress as you'd like it to and you're angry, you can dramatically slam the phone thing in your hand (often called the receiver) into the cradle. When you execute that maneuver you are HANGING UP. If you do it hard enough, it sounds really loud at the other end. You may want to emit a bad word before doing so, just for emphasis. It feels very good.

# *Writing a Letter: From Salutation to the Mailbox*

A letter is another form of communication, a delivery system that used to be the most popular besides CHAT SESSIONS. It requires ink, paper, and, preferably, something to say.

Skip this section if you need remedial help in the alphabet, would like to sing along with Barney, or crave a box of Animal Crackers.

### Starting Your Letter

The first step in writing a letter is to figure out to whom you want to write. If you can't think of someone, zip up your pencil box. But if you have someone in mind, move your hand to the top left side of the paper. Find the top line and write "Dear [person you're writing to]." Whether you write to a friend, relative, or a total stranger, "Dear" is legally required by the False Affection Salutation Act of 1936. Prior to the legislation, the most frequently used salutations were "Hey You!," "Putzboy," and "Lady!"

People like you to use their names when you greet them, rather than your muttered epithet for them. It usually induces them to read through the first line of the letter and sometimes even further. For example, if you're writing to Prince Charles, "Dear Chuck," is preferable to "Dear Shit for Brains."

### Writing Your Letter

Now comes the tough part. You've salutated. Now what? Rare is the letter that starts "Dear Chuck" and is followed by nothing. Here is where your imagination must come through. Write about something that has happened to you, a friend, or family member. If you have no life or family or friends to speak of, write about people on television. Soaps have nearly real people who frequently get sick, die, return as different characters, and marry during the same episode.

**Warning:** As you scribble away, it is better to move your pen to the next line of the paper once there is no space left on the current line. Continuing to write on the same line will cause damage to your desk or other items beside your writing area.

### Ending Your Letter

Finishing your written communication should be easier than wrapping up a *Saturday Night Live* sketch. You can place a period (the small dot that signifies the end of a sentence) wherever you desire but that would give your letter the rhythm of a Bob Dole speech. Periods generally go at the end of a complete sentence. Once you end your thoughts, it's time to say good-bye. But letter writers rarely say "good-bye." They abide by a rider to the False Affection Salutation Act that requires you to be nice to end a letter, too. When ready to close your letter, move your hand from the end of your last sentence to the middle of the next line, where you must write "Sincerely," at the very least. Or "Very truly yours." "Your humble serf" is encouraged to end business correspondence. Then skip down a bit and sign your name.

### Sending Your Letter

This is crucial. No letter is complete until Shit for Brains gets it. Primary to this purpose is folding your letter. You must fold it so that it fits in your envelope, the letter's vessel. You can fold the paper in thirds, halves, quarters, or eighths. Just remember: Shit for Brains is no genius; if you fold it really small, it will take too long for him to unfold it, he will lose patience, and he will probably throw your letter out, even if it means he's won $10 million. Once folded, lick the flap of the letter with your tongue and seal the letter. Then write his address on the front of the envelope. It is almost always required to place a stamp (a small picture surrounded by perforations and a monetary value printed on it. In the United States, that value is 32 cents on the envelope.

# Chapter 5

# JOB SEARCHING FOR REAL DUMMIES

Just as with any worthwhile venture in life, it's necessary to have certain "tools" at your disposal when looking for a job. Those tools include the basics: your resume, your cover letter, and your references. But as with any tools, the sharper yours are, the better the job you'll get.

## *Your Resume*

There are a few key points to remember about a resume. The vast majority of your competitors will submit resumes that are neatly typed on white paper and that all look the same. If you really want that job, be bold, be different, and, most of all, be creative. Remember, it's a competitive world. If you want to compete with the best, you had better be ready to look like you're the best. Note: you don't have to *be* the best—just make them *think* you are.

# *Educational Background*

As with income tax returns, everybody exaggerates a little bit when it comes to resumes. That's just the way it is. Besides, nobody ever gets caught. When was the last time you heard of someone not getting a job because he or she had a minor mistake on their resume—and somebody caught it?

**Example #1:** Suppose the following was your real educational background:

EDUCATION: Harvard Community College, Belle Harbor, Alaska. Associate's degree in physical education.

Wouldn't this edited version look just a little better to the personnel director instead?

EDUCATION: Harvard. Bachelor's degree in physiology and human motion.

**Example #2:** Suppose you were a decent baseball player in high school but never really got around to college. As such, your real resume would read like this:

EDUCATION: Received tuition scholarship to the Dusty Rhodes Baseball Batting Academy, Lollapalooza, Florida.

Now, here's a quick rewrite that's much more impressive and right to the point:

EDUCATION: Rhodes scholar.

**Example #3:** One final sample.

EDUCATION: California School for the Technologically Impaired, San Andreas, California. Earned "Model Railroader's Certificate" in setting up and operating a TYCO train set.

Isn't this simple rewrite a better selling point?

EDUCATION: Cal Tech. Engineering degree.

## Your Cover Letter

Most applicants do their homework by checking on the company. You should be different, creative. Do your homework by checking on the decision maker's personal interests—e.g., bowling, sailing, the WWF, whatever. Then add to your resume that your hobbies include bowling, sailing, the WWF, whatever.

**Note:** This may entail stalking the decision maker for a week or so to ascertain his hobbies and interests. To cover yourself, always be prepared to uncover some potential extortion information.

## Your References

Feel free to list the names of people of such magnitude that the hirer will not only be impressed but will stand absolutely no chance of tracking these people down.

**Example:** if you name a college professor, neighbor, or former coach, of course the hirer will call these people. So why make it easy? Besides, it's much more impressive to put some major league references on your resume. Like:

President Bill Clinton, Warren Buffett, Deion Sanders, Bill Gates. Now, who wouldn't be impressed with that lineup? Even better, who has the time or wherewithal to track these guys down and check on you? Let's see them try:

RECEPTIONIST: Good morning, Mr. Gates's office. How may I help you?

HIRER: Uh, yes, is Mr. Gates in?

RECEPTIONIST: I'm sorry, he's in Japan this week, and then he goes to France. May I give him a message?

HIRER: Oh, okay. My name is Jim Turner and I'm with the human resource department at the Acme Company. I'm calling to check on a reference given to us by a recent job applicant. This applicant said that Mr. Gates was a close personal friend. I'd like Mr. Gates to get back to me about this individual and be so kind as to answer a few questions...

RECEPTIONIST: Well, let's see. I'll add your name to Mr. Gates's list. You're right behind Steve Spielberg, Mother Teresa, Princess Diana, and the Pope. And thank you for calling Microsoft.

## *Special Note for Mid-Career Job Searchers*

These days, it's the rare corporate organization that isn't downsizing so that its stock value can go up. If you find yourself in this situation, be certain you run down to the local Army-Navy store and purchase a variety of multi-colored parachutes. Career counselors claim that these parachutes will come in handy if you decide to, say, jump off a building or bridge—i.e., the various colors make the chute easier to spot in the river below when they retrieve what's left of you.

# Chapter 6

# RELIGION FOR REAL DUMMIES

• • • • • • • • • • • • • • • • • • • • • • • • • • • • • • • • • • • •

*In this chapter*
- ▶ Jackie Mason: Advice from the real Jewish pope
- ▶ Best prices for cleaning religious garments
- ▶ Cleaning your stained glass

• • • • • • • • • • • • • • • • • • • • • • • • • • • • • • • • • • • •

## *How Well Do You Know Religion?*

At lot of people claim that they're religious, that they follow the Scriptures or live by the Koran. So you think you know religion? Try this (answers at end of chapter):

1. Is it kosher to keep your yarmulkes in your socks drawer?

2. What is the ceiling on the number of pastries allowed on a Viennese table?

3. Who was the best cinematic Christ?

4. At what times are the Pope's feet allowed to touch the ground?

5. What is the first stanza of "Dominique"?

6. What was Whoopi Goldberg's nun name in the *Sister Act* films?

7. What brand shoes did Anthony Quinn wear in *Shoes of the Fisherman?*

8. Can you be baptized in a desert if there is no water?

9. At a briss—the Jewish circumcision ritual—is pastrami or corned beef preferred?

10. Whose cousin is the rock 'n roller Jerry Lee Lewis?
(a) Jimmy Swaggart (b) Noman Vincent Peale (c) Jim J.
Bullock (d) Jim Bakker (e) Rev. Ike?

11. When Martin Luther hammered his 95 theses to the cas-
tle church door, did he use finishing, common, roofing, or
masonry nails?

---

**1.** Kosher? In fact, preferred. **2.** 27, including rice pudding. **3.** The modern view: Willem Dafoe. **4.** When he lands, of course. **5.** "Dominque/Dominique/Dominique/Dominique." **6.** Sister Mary Clarence Thomas. **7.** Converse Chuck Cooper. **8.** Didn't you bring Evian for the trip? **9.** Actually, tongue. **10.** (c)**11.** Common.

---

# How to Choose Your Religion

You're a lapsed Catholic. A doubting Protestant. A plotzed
Jew. A harried Hare Krishna. A dead-again born-again. You
want a new faith. There are four things to consider in
choosing a religion: the leader, the hat, the book, and the
holidays.

### Choosing the Leader for You

Unlike a president, an alderman, or a union shop steward,
you can't elect your religious leaders. Religions are not
democracies. Leaders are prechosen for you by small
groups of men in long gowns, God, or a puff of smoke. The
leaders come from a broad spectrum of studies and backgrounds. Some are legendary, some alive, some currently
dead but often seen in statues, and some are seen playing
cards on velvet backgrounds.

**Tips:** How to Choose Your Religious Leader:

• Does the leader require prayer at inopportune times?

• Does he make you laugh?

- Is the leader's Good Book really good? Did it make a good movie?

- Does he require that you wear religious garb while sleeping?

- Is his music good enough to dance to?

- Does his science fiction work measure up to Ray Bradbury's?

**Who's the best leader for you?**
- **Roman Catholics:** John Paul II, Andrew Greeley, John F. Kennedy, Jr.

- **Buddhists:** Buddha Gautama, Dalai Lama, Dolly Levi, Richard Gere

- **Jews:** Menachem Schneerson, Jackie Mason, Ed Koch, Steven Spielberg

- **Muslims:** Mohammed, Muhammad Ali, Louis Farrakhan

- **Protestants:** Archbishop of Canterbury, Pat Robertson

- **Hindus:** Swami Vivekananda, Maharishi Mahesh Yogi, Yogi Bear

- **Mormons:** Joseph Smith, Brigham Young, 7'7" New Jersey Net Shawn Bradley (someone you can look up to)

- **Scientology:** L. Ron Hubbard, Tom Cruise, John Travolta

### *Choosing the Right Religious Headgear*

As a rule, you don't get to wear snappy religious hats if you're in a church, mosque, temple, or Madison Square Garden. The leader gets first dibs on headwear, and the best you usually get is a skullcap or yarmulke. There is no best hat, just the best hat for you:

**Miter:** Tallest of all. Comes in several colors. Looks great on the Pope. Bishops wear simple miters but want the cardinal's precious miter. Perfect conversation piece at communion parties.

**Biretta:** Square cap with three corners is a must-wear for Roman Catholics.

**Yarmulkes:** Satin, silk, wool, cotton. Very flexible. Can be in solid colors or have designs as varied as a Jerusalem street scene or the Smurfs. Jews have them, and Catholics wear them but call them skullcaps.

**Tonsure:** Not a hat per se, but the shaved head is affected by monks and Buddhists. Sometimes accessorized with a ponytail.

### Selecting the Right Religious Book

They all have lofty, intimidating names and all sell very well. But what distinguishes one from the other? Length. The longer the book, the more history you have to pay attention to, the more rules you have to obey, and, most important, the longer your service will be. The book you choose also depends entirely on what you want to derive from the religion you select:

**Bible I Old Testament:** A good book with many familiar first names but very few last names. Hard to remember the whole cast without a program.

**Bible II Old & New Testaments:** Longer version, starring Jesus Christ as the Savior.

**Torah:** Shorter, more concise. Usually comes in a scroll. Read from back to front.

**Koran:** The book of Islam. Longest one-volume religious book, except for 50-volume collection of Hindu texts. Cliff Notes unavailable.

**Book of Common Prayer's hymnal:** Songbook for all sorts of Protestants. Prayer arranged by Nelson Riddle.

**Book of Mormon:** Playbook for Brigham Young's football team. And polygamy.

**Dianetics:** Sci-fi.

**Kama Sutra:** Va-va-voom!

### *Choosing by the Holiday*

Above all, which religion has the best holidays?

Christians lead the way with the familiar biggies Christmas and Easter.

Chanukah is a week-long extravaganza for the Jewish faith. Jews even have an eight-day candelabra to commemorate the holiday. For very religious Jews and grade school students, Jews have a broad selection of day-off holidays, including Passover, Rosh Hashanah, Simchats Torah and Shavuot.

Muslims have the month-long Ramadan, which is a mixed-blessing holiday. Sure, it's a month-long celebration of the revelation of the Koran to Mohammed. But Muslims have to fast from dwan to dusk for thirty days. It's no picnic, but it is recommended by Jenny Craig.

Jews only have to fast on one day, Yom Kippur, but get to eat by sundown. Unlike Muslims like Hakeem Olajuwon, who can pray at home and play in arenas around the country during Ramadan, observant Jews must spend their fast day in synagogues, where no basketball is allowed.

# *Keeping Your Religious Articles Clean*

If cleanliness is next to godliness, then you'd better keep your yarmulke dry-cleaned, your skullcap spiffy, and your crucifix brightly polished.

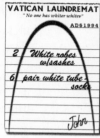

**VATICAN LAUNDREMAT**
*"No one has whiter whites"*
AD61994

| 2 | *White robes w/sashes* |
| 6 | *pair white tube socks* |

*John*

Most religious articles are delicate and should be hand-washed, on the delicate cycle.

**Beware:** If you're a cardinal, don't launder your white Jockey briefs with the red satin robe. Not even in cold water. Stay away from Woolite. That robe is one of your most valuable dainties and must be handled with the utmost respect.

**Tip:** Launder your scapular *very* carefully.

**Beware:** If you don't, you'll go to hell.

Here is what the Pope pays for his dry cleaning at the Vatican Laundremat—which has offered a special Piusizing service for an extra charge since 140—if he really paid. One of the Pope's perks of course, is free laundry. It's good to be the Pope.

| | | |
|---|---|---|
| St. Peter's Miter $23.50 | Alb 11.50 | Ring of the Fisherman 5.00 |
| Road Trip Miter 25.00 | Cincture 2.50 | Bracelet of the Lobsterman 8.00 |
| Skullcap (zuccheto) 3.75 | Chasuble 18.50 | |
| Amice 10.00 | Pope Shoes (rented) 3.50 | Satin Boxers 7.95 |
| Cassock 11.25 | Papal Nikes (official footwear of Air Pontiff) 1.50 | Shoes of Stan the Man 16.75 |
| Stole 8.50 | | |
| Cope 9.25 | Staff gratis | |

# Cleaning Grime from Your Stained Glass

If cleanliness is next to godliness, then someone has to clean those stained windows, especially after they get egged on Halloween. If Allah himself were walking toward your mosque and you couldn't see him because there was some unsightly grime on the windows, think what you'd miss. So here are the best methods for cleaning your stained glass:

### Recommended cleaners:

- Windex

- Fantastic

- Didi 7 (available only through TV offers)

### Recommended tools:

- Sponge

- Squeegee

- Dry rags

### Recommended usage:

- Wet window with cleaner

- Wipe around with sponge

- Clear off with squeegee

- Dry with rag

To clean stained glass on Saturdays, when observant Jews can only observe and pray, synagogues are urged to hire a Shabbos squeegee goy—that is, a non-Jew squeegee professional.

# Choosing the Right Confessional

If you've committed any sins, and you probably have if you're currently alive, you may feel a need to confess them. Some people confess to their spouses, their children, their shrinks, their pets, their bowling buddies, or Oprah. But religious confession is something different. And if you are going to people confess your sins in a small, enclosed room with a priest in the middle and some other poor schlep on the other side, you should consider the following:

- Is the confessional air-conditioned, and, if not, do you at least get a battery-operated fan to use during summer or steamy confessions? Does it come with a combined television-VCR?

- Can you sit on a chair during the other person's confession, or must you kneel the entire time on a bar, as the traditional confession requires? Does the church offer a small stool?

- Are you allowed to wear knee pads?

- While you await the other penitents' sins-of-all-sins wrap-up, does the church offer a Walkman to listen to Madonna's rendition of religious psalms?

- The first time you confess, either as a child or an adult, can be frightening. Does your church offer a video to those who've never confessed before? Like _Barney Goes to Church and Confesses to Coveting Baby Bop_?

- Many newcomers don't know you have to wait until the priest lowers his little door before you start confessing. Does the priest say, "Hit it," to start your confession going?

# Chapter 7

# TELEVISION FOR REAL DUMMIES

Very few things in life are as important as learning how to watch television effectively. Yet sadly, each year tens of thousands of Americans never learn this important skill properly. And rather than confess to lacking an understanding of this essential vehicle of societal communication, these poor souls try to live a lie, faking that they know how to get the most out of their television sets.

## *Getting Plugged into the Television Age*

All of the following discussion assumes that you, in fact, have a television set and are somewhat familiar with its basic operation. In order to gain maximum enjoyment and endless hours of amusement from your television, you should keep these basic instructions in mind:

1. Sit in front of the TV set. You'd be amazed at how many people sit behind the set, making viewing both difficult and skewed.

2. Sit at least fifteen feet away from the TV screen. Feel free to adjust your home viewing area by picking up your chair and moving it accordingly.

3. Learn how to adjust the sound. This can be tricky, since you have to find a button or knob that's labelled VOLUME—not SOUND. In the dictionary, VOLUME refers to "quantities of units." But here, VOLUME refers to controlling the loudness of the sound emanating from your set.

## *Look Out for This Common Mistake!*

If you're watching TV and the picture on your screen looks uncannily like your building lobby, and not much is happening except for passers-by who look an awful lot like your neighbors, chances are you're watching a closed-circuit TV monitor. This can be confusing, since closed-circuit TV does resemble a number of popular sitcoms on regular TV. But this, in fact, is not real TV.

## *Is Television Bad for Your Health?*

Eat as much as you like when watching TV! According to a recent scientific study conducted by Dr. Sofa Tuber at La-Z-Boy University, your brain's hypothalamus will respond to whatever activity you're watching on television. Thus, if you're watching a running marathon, your body will also burn up thousands of calories as you watch the runners go mile after mile. (It should be pointed out, however, that most of the subjects in Dr. Tuber's study chose to watch bridge on TV, which expends no more than three calories an hour. As a result, most of the subjects reported significant weight gains.)

Use television to improve other parts of your life as well, such as your vocabulary. Up until a few years ago, some very useful and functional words had been banned from TV. Thankfully, you can now learn the use of such proper nouns as "scumbag" and "asshole" by simply tuning into network prime-time TV.

## *Getting the Most Out of Your VCR*

Some people who own a TV also own a VCR, which allows one to videotape a TV program in order to view it at a later time. Others, however, own only a VCR without a TV. That's not such a good idea, because you usually need a TV in order to gain maximum usage out of a VCR unless, of course, you want to tape a "film noir".

# Your Television Troubleshooter's Guide

IF YOUR SCREEN IS BLACK...check to see whether
your set is actually plugged in and that the "on" switch is turned to the
"on" position.

IF ALL YOU SEE IS THE OTHER SIDE OF THE ROOM...
simply turn your chair around. Note that the television was originally behind you.
You are now facing it and should be able to see the picture clearly.

IF YOU SEE PICTURES BUT DON'T HEAR ANYTHING...check the volume knob.
Turn it up.

IF YOU SEE PICTURES AND HEAR SOUNDS, BUT YOUR TELEVISION SET IS
TURNED OFF...check to see if you are taking any hallucinogenic drugs. If you are,
stop taking them. If you aren't, check with your local psychiatrist as to why you're
hearing voices and seeing pictures without the benefit of a television.

IF YOU'RE WATCHING A PROGRAM CALLED *SATURDAY NIGHT LIVE* BUT
YOU'RE NOT LAUGHING...relax. The show stopped being funny about ten
years ago.

# Chapter 8

# DEATH FOR REAL DUMMIES

Statistics show that everyone and everything grows old and dies, except maybe *Saturday Night Live*. Death, then, is undoubtedly the most widely experienced activity in life. You can't go a day without hearing about somebody dying. Obituaries are filled with dead people. So are retirement communities. While dying is very active, being dead is much more passive. It is very final and can only rarely be altered.

## Commonplace Signs That Someone Is Dead

Mail is not picked up for at least three months. Anyone who does not respond to eighteen consecutive requests from Publishers Clearinghouse solicitations must be dead. Or she doesn't have her best polyester dress out of the cleaners to meet the Prize Patrol.

The person is said to have been "assassinated," which can only mean a famous politician or pope. Regular people are never assassinated, even if they were in the Jacuzzi with the violently killed famous person. The non-famous person will then be reported to have died in a violent bathing accident.

Not breathing for more than six hours means a person is no longer holding out for a better deal. Make double certain that the person has not been holding his breath all that time by pulling up an eyelid. If that starts him singing Andrew Lloyd Webber's score to that Sanskrit oldie, "Mahabharata," chances are he's alive.

## Suicide Tips

1. Be a contestant in the Himalayan luge on ESPN's "Extreme Games."

2. Blow-dry your hair while taking a bubble bath.

3. Botulism from cans of Bubba Gump shrimp gumbo, shrimp creole, shrimp jumbo shrimp parmigiana, shrimp scampi, shrimp cocktail, shrimp Waldorf Salad, shrimp William Howard Taft, shrimp Where's Waldo, shrimp Oscar, shrimp Felix, or shrimp Ted Kaczyinski.

4. Watch a marathon of Pauly Shore movies. Most deaths usually occur midway through _Jury Duty_.

5. Eat only British beef.

## Statements That Will Bring Dr. Jack Kevorkian to Your House

- "I've fallen and I can't get up."

- "Give me liberty or give me death."

- "Darn that hangnail."

- "Should I buy a car with two exhaust pipes?"

# Preparing for Death

**Your Underwear:** Your scanties are too often overlooked. Say you get gunned down, you slump inert while on your aunt's plastic-covered sofa, or you drop like a stone while jogging, even though you've written a bestseller on jogging. The paramedics pick you up and cut through your clothes to resuscitate you. What do they find but dirty underwear? Or soiled Depends? What your mother said is 100 percent true: Clean underwear makes a better impression than ragged underthings. Besides, doctors avoid treating the patient who's worn those cheap briefs for an entire week without changing them.

For men, silk boxers are preferred. For women, Victoria's Secret has a lovely, little-known line of silk and satin coffin-wear.

# Estate Planning

**Your Living Will:** Doctors are always trying all sorts of things to extend life. You may want them to do everything possible to keep your heart pumping, your lungs breathing, your liver livering, and your pancreas doing whatever it is your pancreas does.

**Warning:** Doctors are liable to cut you open and vacuum your intestines with the latest Hoover XKE Colon Suck-It-Clean to keep you alive unless you specify against it. A typical living will goes like this, and can be prepared by a properly trained lawyer, hardware salesman, bus driver, or department store Santa:

I [state your name], being of sound mind and body—well, actually I'm feeling pretty crappy—wish, in the unlikely event that my organs stop playing, to continue to have WATER unless BUCKLER'S NONALCOHOLIC BEER is available.

I, [state your name], wish to continue to be given OXYGEN in the event that I can't breathe on my own, but wouldn't mind, for the occasional chuckle, that HELIUM be pumped into my lungs, for what is a near death experience unless I can sound like Tiny Tim?

I, [state your name], wish to be kept alive in the event that I am declared brain  dead or lower-intestine-dead or dead-as-Jacob Marley dead, for as long as I can continue to get generic medication on my HMO prescription card for the $5 co-payment.

I, [state your name], figure, what the hell.

**Tip:** Specify a codicil—a legal P.S.—that states if your HMO doesn't cover all this stuff, the plug must be pulled.

## *Your Will*

You got nothing, you don't need a will. You think anybody wants your Cracker Jack toys?

 You got money, spend it. Leave nothing behind. If you're constitutionally unwilling to spend while you're living, make out a will with one provision: All the money goes to the best-danged funeral ever. Dancing girls or Chippendale's men. Janet Jackson or Michael Bolton. Stiller and Meara. Alan King. Wayne and Schuster. Señor Wences ("You are dead? You are niiiice!"). Flying Wallendas. Sitting Wallendas. Vikki Carr. Hold a funeral in the stadium of your choice. Hire a top-notch pastry chef. The best cold cuts.

Sure, you won't be there, but won't you love to know that the child you hate, the one who stood like a geek waving outside the *Today Show* studios on the day of your stroke, is watching his inheritance pass before him in the form of pastrami sandwiches and Wayne Newton signing "Danke Schoen"?

If you insist on preparing a will, follow these tips:

- If you've got at least $600,000 in cash, get married. Now. No matter how old you are. Mail away for a Filipino bride.

- Waylay an Afghan cabbie. Or give Anna Nicole Smith a call.

- If you follow neither of these steps, here are the tax penalties your estate will incur if you don't plan ahead:

## VALUE OF ESTATE FEDERAL TAX RATE & OTHER PENALTIES

| Value of Estate | Tax Rate & Penalty |
|---|---|
| $ 600,000 - 750,000 | 37% Must be buried in a grapefruit crate. |
| 750,001 - 1,000,000 | 39% No pillow or blanket in casket. |
| 1,000,001 - 1,250,000 | 41% Burial wrapped in Holiday Inn towel. |
| 1,250,001 - 1,500,000 | 43% Naked burial. |
| 1,500,001 - 2,000,000 | 45% Donald Trump gives your eulogy. |
| 2,000,001 - 2,500,000 | 49% Ivana Trump gives your eulogy. |
| 2,500,001 - 3,000,000 | 53% Become Dennis Rodman's boy toy. |
| 3,000,001 - 10,000,000 | 55% Become Dennis Rodman's girl toy |
| 10,000,001 - 21,040,000 | 60% Co-star in a Charlie Sheen movie. |

# Communicating with Other Folks in the Afterlife

### DeadNet Basics

Prior to doing anything interesting on the DeadNet, you must die, be interred, and have your soul rise. You'll need a connection to others on the DeadNet and a fixed idea of the things you want to say. You'll also need names and forwarding addresses.

> **HOUDINI**
> 1874-1926
> THE WORLD'S
> GREATEST
> ESCAPE ARTIST
> WWW.ESCAPE.COM

### DeadNet Access Services, Databases and Home Pages

With the correct connections, you can pick up all the information you want for eternity. Consider the following:

**dole.mort@AmericaOffLine** — Where to replay past presidential defeats from Aaron Burr to Robert Dole. Downloading naked photos of Hubert Humphrey from the not-so-secret files of J. Edgar Hoover is a popular activity.

**http://www.corpuserve** — Up-to-the-minute tips for the newly reincarnated, from the newest clothing styles and the highest cholesterol dishes available, to an easy-to-use program that tracks down departed friends you've lost touch with.

**nobreath.inert@Departigy** — An index of every death, updated by the minute. Actual video and audio available to watch live funerals. Special service allows for funeral replays back to 1962.

**(yourname)@Necro.extinct** — This is your Necromail service, allowing you to send messages to anyone linked to N-Mail. Exchange thoughts on pillow maintenance, best places for tacos in heaven or hell, and purgatory's best urologists.

# Chapter 9

# TIME MANAGEMENT FOR REAL DUMMIES

In order to manage your time, you first have to understand how much of it you have left. And it doesn't look pretty.

## *Figuring Out How Much Time You Have Left*

Here's an easy and delightful way to measure your mortality—when you can expect to die. (All measurements are based on professional actuarial tables, assuming 60 seconds in a minute, 60 minutes in an hour, 24 hours in a day and so on.)

**If You're 40**…you have 35 years to go. Or more accurately, since there are only 31,536,000 seconds in a year, you have only about 31.5 million seconds times 35 years to live, or 1.1325 billion seconds.

Sounds like a lot, doesn't it? Well, once you subtract a third of that time for sleep, plus all the time you waste every day eating fatty foods, watching stupid sitcoms on TV, sitting on the can, and chatting idly on the phone, you can see that you have but a few mere seconds of life left. The only good news here is that you're not 60, 70, or 80.

**If You're 60**…take a good, long look at yourself in the mirror. Not a pretty sight, is it? Just imagine what you're going to look like in ten or—gulp!—20 years.

**If You're 70**…start reducing the clutter in your life by throwing out the clocks you have. Why do you need to keep reminding yourself that the seconds continue to tick away?

**If You're 80**…start figuring out a way to take it all with you. Now! Try starting your own Web site. Maybe you can somehow transfer all of your earthly assets there, and later figure out how to plug into the World Wide Web from the other side of the River Styx (see chapter 8 now!!)

## How to Best Utilize the Precious Hours You Have Left...

Let's get back to the work a day world. Only then can one start dealing effectively with managing one's time. Again, let's start with the basics:

# A typical business day:

| | |
|---|---|
| 9 hours | for sleeping |
| 1 hour | for getting dressed, shower, reading paper, etc. |
| 2 hours | for commuting to and from work |
| 1 hour | for catching up on yesterday's work (phone calls, memos, etc.) |
| 1 hour | for boring, mandatory meetings |
| 1/2 hour | for catching up on office gossip |
| 1/2 hour | of uninterrupted work |
| 1 1/2 hours | for lunch |
| 1 hour | for catching up on the morning's missed phone calls |
| 1 hour | for another boring, mandatory meeting |
| 1/2 hour | for catching up on office gossip |
| 1/2 hour | to go through classified ads, talk with headhunters, etc. |
| 1 hour | to daydream, read the newspaper, do the crossword puzzle, call friends |
| 1 hour | for dinner |
| 1 hour | to cope with daily annoyances in life (mowing the lawn, dealing with life insurance agents, relatives, family obligations, etc.) |
| 3 hours | for playing with kids, watching TV, paying bills, playing softball/drinking beer, doing kids' homework, servicing the spouse |
| **Total: 24 hours** | **a perfectly time-managed day, with little wasted time or effort. It's what life is all about!** |

## How to Tell Time

The general public is always amazed to discover that there are, in fact, two ways of telling time. There's the traditional (and more difficult) way of attempting to read a clock, and there's the modern way of reading a digitalized clock.

**The Traditional:** In order to be able to tell time, you have to first know that traditional clocks have hour and minute hands that rotate in a clockwise direction. Warning: If your clock has its hour and minute hands going in the opposite direction, then you're most likely trapped in a time machine and going backward.

**The Modern Way:** An entire generation has grown up weaned on digital clocks. This requires being able to count to 60 but no higher. It also requires an instinctive ability to tell morning hours from evening hours.

## How to Manage Your Time

If the above chart is similar to yours, then it's obvious that you know how to make the most of your limited days on earth. If, however, you're not up to speed on saving time at the office, then perhaps the following tips will help.

## Tips for Saving Time at the Office

**How to get a gabber off the phone:** In a cheery but firm voice, tell him or her that you have to get off the line because: "It's been great chatting with you, but unfortunately, the office building is on fire and the firemen have ordered me to vacate the premises immediately."

**Buy a "shave-a-minute"** clock that deletes a few minutes off each hour you work: Instead of working a 60-minute hour, you'll be working only 55 minutes an hour. That saves 40 minutes a day, or 200 minutes a week. Note: When your shave-a-minute starts to show that it's 5:30 p.m. and it's really only lunchtime, reset it and start again.

## *How to Tell Day From Night*

This is an amazing printed simulation of Day. And this is an amazing printed simulation of Night.

**NIGHT**    **DAY**

Note: This concept is not as simple as it seems. For example, you could be in a room that's lit up, even though it's really night outside. Likewise, you could be in a very dark room, such as a broom closet or basement and, judging from the lack of bright sunlight, you would assume it's night. In fact, if you walked outside, it could be quite bright.

If you don't feel comfortable making these judgment calls by yourself, understand that it takes a little time and experience. Don't be discouraged if you find yourself becoming confused.

# Chapter 10

# ETIQUETTE FOR REAL DUMMIES

Is it possible for the Real Dummy to be perfectly mannered, to know how to behave in every possible social and business situation? Of course not. Real Dummies are slow to educate, even slower to train, but that's why you're *Real Dummies!* Etiquette comes through long days of training, of learning to tell a fork from a spoon, and of understanding the difference between a get-well card and a sympathy note. But if you follow these instructions, you should be able to navigate ordering at a McDonald's or gracefully apologize for cutting the cheese at a cocktail party.

## *Reaching for What You Deserve*

**Problem:** You're the thirteenth person at a table that really seats twelve—an unwelcome guest at a dinner party hosted by person number twelve. You've got perhaps three-quarters of a space for yourself, and nobody is talking to you. You're eating a very dry steak that begs for Adolph's meat tenderizer, which is sitting unused halfway down the table. You try to get someone's attention to pass it, but no one does.
Is it correct to reach over two or three people, or even get up and walk over to the other end of the table to get it?

**Solution:** Get that tenderizer by any means necessary, my friend. Crawl over a few people, if you must. There's nothing worse than the host of a party ruining perfectly good beef by overcooking it. I'm sure your host never asked you how you wanted your steak cooked. Perhaps he or she likes it burnt! So go ahead, step on a few laps in your quest to beef up your beef. And if the Adolph's ain't on the table, feel free to know that Real Dummies Etiquette allows you to walk, without permission, to the host's refrigerator and select the condiment of your choice. Empty the spice rack if need be.

## When to Forcibly Restrain Your Flatulent Instincts

**Problem:** Frequently you're faced with when to fart and when not to fart. Is it ever socially correct to flatulate in the presence of others? How best to acknowledge when you accidentally, ahem, break wind?

**Solution:** Job interviews and first sexual encounters are the only times to forcibly hold in farts. There are no other times. To best acknowledge to others the wind you have quite clearly broken, it is proper to say, "Ooooh, baby I love it."

## Flushing Your Co-Worker the Proper Way

**Problem:** You've just entered the bathroom in your office, and the co-worker walking from the urinal or stall has not flushed. Do you ignore this sin against sanitation or say something?

**Solution:** If there's one motto that defines Real Dummies Etiquette, it is: "Never let any unflushed toilet go unremarked." The best you can say is, "When you pee at home, do you flush?" If that doesn't embarrass him or her, do your business, flush in a dramatic manner (provide play-by-play, if you desire) and leave. Later, scrawl rude graffiti in bathroom stalls about your no-flush co-worker.

## *When to Expose Yourself*

**Problem:** The world is so informal these days. Everybody talks about everything and what's discussed over lunch with a friend or co-worker is laid out to Geraldo or Maury. Are there any subjects that cannot be broached to someone?

**Solution:** First, let us remember the subjects that any Real Dummy knows are fair game during any situation from a job interview to a friendly bridge game: age, medical condition, homosexuality, income, fertility, recent deaths, race, religion, and politics. There is actually only one subject that should not be brought up by considerate people speaking in decent company: Rush Limbaugh naked.

## *Guideposts for Thank-You Notes*

**Problem:** You've just gotten married and need to know which of your wedding gifts require thank-yous and which don't.

**Solution:** You'll be surprised to learn that not all gifts, cash or otherwise, require a thank-you note. Here are two easy measuring sticks: One, all cash gifts of $100 or more get a thank-you. Two, all other gifts worth at least $100 get thank-you's, too. If you're in doubt about a physical gift's value, call the store. If you don't know the store, but it looks cheap, forget about it. If the giver of the cheap gift hints around about not getting a thank-you, tell him you never got his gift and wondered what kind of a cheap bastard would come to your wedding without something worth $100.

## *Showing Gratitude for a Rotten Gift*

**Problem:** You're the recipient of a hideously ugly wedding gift that is worth more than $100. How do you politely write a thank-you note?

**Solution:** Here's the easiest way to get through this sticky moment. Anybody who sends something that inappropriate deserves to know that his or her gift was the one that was returned:

*Dear Friends:*
*Thank you so much for the satin pig so graciously stuffed with artichoke hearts. Unfortunately, it was the seventh one we received (everyone seems to have seen* Babe *this year), and we hope you don't mind that we exchanged it for something we really want.*

*Love and ham hocks, etc.*

## *When to Tip a Bathroom Attendant*

**Problem:** We are again in the bathroom. You have handled everything on your own, and can pump your own soap and wipe your own hands with the paper towels. But an attendant is there, imposing his or her services on you. Must you tip him or her and if so how much?

**Solution:** There is only one instance that obliges the Real Dummy to tip this type of person. Unless the attendant truly provides a real service—that is, helps you do your business by emitting helpful tinkling sounds—he or she deserves no remuneration. **Bonus:** If the attendant isn't looking or is otherwise occupied handing a towel to another person who could have gotten the towel on his own, feel free to lift some loose bills from the attendant's tip tray.

# *Tipping Solutions for All Occasions*

**Problem:** While it seems like everybody wants a tip, service is slipping everywhere. What standards of tipping are recommended?

**Solution:** Dummies never tip unless the service merits it. We've always felt that five percent is an appropriate tip for good service, ten percent tops. So those waiters had better do well to get our hard-earned nickel for every dollar of the bill. Here is a guide to what to give to a variety of greedy service providers:

| OCCUPATION | GRATUITY |
| --- | --- |
| Bartender | A dirty joke for every drink |
| Busboys | Tell him you gave the waiter a fat gratuity intended for you to share. |
| Checkroom Attendants | The check. And a smile, of course. |
| Headwaiters | Nothing. Zip. How much work is it to seat you, hand you the menus, and say, "Enjoy your meal"? Hey, I work for a living, buddy! |
| Wine steward | Just say, "Ummm boy, that was good booze" |
| Skycaps | 25 cents per bag of luggage over 250 lbs |
| Hotel bellperson | Ditto |
| Hotel maid | Whatever loose change you have left at the end of your stay |
| Garage attendant | Instructions on cleaning that black stuff from under their nails |
| Cab drivers | A deluxe-size can of deodorant |
| Movie theater ushers | All the loose Jujubes and popcorn on theater floors |
| Golf course caddie | Your biggest, meatiest, dirtiest divots |
| Letter carrier | Even though the U.S. Postal Service says not to tip the mailpeople, give yours at least $100. Postal employees must be made happy at any and all cost. Remember, peel back the Postal Service emblem and you see an NRA emblem |

# Chapter 11

# PARENTING FOR REAL DUMMIES

There is no greater thrill than to become a parent and pass all of your genetic and sociological faults and flaws on to the next generation.

There's also a downside to parenthood, however. Becoming a mom or dad brings on a personal acceleration toward middle age, including a constant loss of sleep, unwanted worries, tremendous debt beyond your wildest imagination, and more!

But don't fret. There are quick and simple way to make the parenting transition a little easier to deal with. For example, dealing with the expense:

1. Disposable diapers are expensive. But disposable diapers don't have to be changed as often as most parents think! That's a myth foistered by the makers of these disposable diapers. Today's standard diaper can easily last one to two weeks before having to be disposed of.

2. Forget all that baby chow. Baby food not only tastes terrible (taste it for yourself—would you eat it?), but it comes in those little bottles and, again, is very expensive. Serve babies real food—pizza, donuts, candy bars, etc. Not only is it cheaper, it's much easier to handle and, besides, it's what all kids love to eat.

3. Getting tired of those weekly trips to see the pediatrician because your kid has a sore throat or simple fever? Look, the truth is, kids do get sick, but they normally bounce back the next day. Just make certain you have a jumbo, 50-pound bag of "Tylenol for Kids" on hand, and you can handle just about any childhood malady. This strategy will shave 70 percent off your yearly medical bills.

## *How to Discipline Your Child Effectively... and Painlessly*

Being a parent means sometimes having to be the disciplinarian. Kids without discipline grow up to be spoiled brats, so it's important to learn right away how to fulfill this parental function. Here are some common scenarios:

**Example:** Your darling eight-year-old boy is running out of control in the living room and accidentally takes a slap shot at one of your priceless lamps. As you bend over to pick up the pieces and shards of shattered lamp, you realize that you ought to say something to little Johnny.

**The Wrong Way:** "Jonathan, now do you understand that I, as your parent and as an adult, do not approve of your roguish behavior? After all, running around the house while brandishing a hockey stick can only cause problems and damage to material things. Now, this is important: Please recognize that I still very much love you, and that you're a truly special, gifted child. But that being said, I don't approve of your aggressive behavior when it comes to smashing lamps.

"Furthermore, perhaps your aberrant behavior is more symptomatic of a deeper emotional problem—maybe it's a reflection of my shortcomings as a parent. And to that end, I should be apologizing to you for my failure to teach you right from wrong. In fact, the more I think about it, the more I realize that perhaps I'm the one who should be punished here. After all, who can blame an eight-year-old? How can one so young be expected to know how to behave, unless he is taught by a supposedly fully mature adult? Indeed, I ask you, I beg you—can you ever find it in your heart to forgive me? I promise to do better as your parent in the future."

**The Right Way:** "Jonathan, do you realize that the lamp you just smashed is your grandmother's absolute favorite? That lamp has been in the family for over five generations, and your grandmother always talks so fondly of it. It reminds her of her mother and all the special moments they had together. Now, as you know, your grandmother is in frail health, and the last thing she said to me this morning was, 'Whatever you do, please make certain that my favorite lamp is always protected and cherished. Why, without that lamp, I don't know if I would have the strength to go on. It's the only thing in life that means anything to me.'

"So, Jonathan, perhaps you understand just how important that lamp is. Now, do you have to say anything on your behalf before I make you go upstairs and call Grandma on the phone to tell her what you did to her lamp?"

## *Nature v. Nurture: The Controversy Is Resolved*

Although it wasn't widely reported by the media, this age-old controversy was recently put to rest. The Harvard University Center for Human Development, after several years of intensive research, announced last spring that every child's personality is determined as a mix of 85 percent nature (meaning strictly genetic influences) and 15 percent nurture (meaning one's environmental and sociological influences).

In other words, your children are not only going to look like you, they're going to act like you, think like you, and be just like you—only in a younger version.

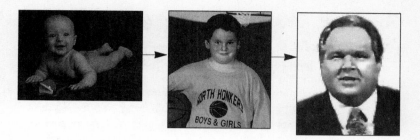

Too bad. That beautiful, blond-haired, little wisp of a child will grow up to be bald, gap-toothed, fat slob with an IQ of about 90, lots of hair on his back, and a beer gut. And there's nothing you can do about it.

### *Developmental Time Line for Parents*

Parents always want to know how their precious ones match up with other kids their age. Here's a quick way to see how your child is progressing:

| | |
|---|---|
| Six months | — Looks cute and cuddly. Smiles a lot and poops a lot. |
| Nine months | — Begins to walk and talk, saying "Ma-Ma" and "Da-Da." |
| Twelve months | — Can talk in complete sentences. Can take several steps. |
| Eighteen months | — Can spell simple words like pneumonia, celluloid, and catechism. |
| Twenty-four months | — Can dribble a basketball with both hands and make decent bounce passes. |
| Age Three | — Has read biographies of all the American presidents and has memorized the Bill of Rights. |
| Age Five | — Having learned geometry and algebra, should be starting basic calculus. |
| Age Six | — Totally fluent in English, Spanish, and German. |

# Kids: A Troubleshooter's Guide for Parents

All moms and dads run into occasional roadblocks when it comes to raising their children. It makes no difference who you are, where you live, or how much money you make. All parents need a little help every so often. Here's a brief sampling of the kinds of situations that many parents are confronted with:

Your twelve-year-old son is caught painting swastikas on a school wall. As an aspiring parental dummy, you should:
— Sit down and explain to him why the defacing of public property is wrong.
— Stick up for your child and challenge the school's authority to restrain your child's freedom of speech.
— Consider moving to Argentina.

Your sixteen-year-old daughter's role model is Madonna. You should:
— Make her sit down and listen to Madonna's albums over and over again.
— Explain to her what a skank Madonna really is.
— Get her an agent.

Your son, who's a budding 7´2˝ basketball star, says he would prefer to drop basketball and study to become a doctor. You should:
— Applaud him for his humanitarian goals.
— Explain to him what an economic blow it would be to become a doctor when he could make millions putting a ball through a hoop.
— Get him an agent.

You walk in on your fourteen-year-old daughter smoking a joint. You should:
— Call the cops and have her dragged off in handcuffs.
— Encourage her entrepreneurial instincts by showing her how to market and distribute the drug to her friends.
— Ask her if she has any more she can share with you.

Your fourteen-year-old daughter proudly tells you over dinner one evening that she's gay. You should:
— Explain to her that you don't care about her sexual orientation, as long as she's happy.
— Explain to her that she was adopted and that you're not her biological mother.
— Explain to her that she's a lot like her father.

# Chapter 12

# THE INTERNET FOR REAL DUMMIES

The Internet is a vast gov/netw.ork of on-line networks led by mice. //If you keep pressing your. mouse, you can keep travel.ing in cyber//space. It is \\a:communications marvel that allows you. t.o. communicate with alt.//virtually any.one on the html/http//// planet and get access. to information ed. you never.com thought you'd need.soc. The Internet has a v.ery peculiar form of gramm.mar.com alt.syntax//.com and punc/tuatio/n that requires the inadvertent and hel.ter.skelter use of perio.ds.alt// and slash/////es that otherwise make.no sense.sci to anyone but those who // snarf stu.ff in cyber//.space.edu.

## Who Runs the Internet?

Much has been made of the democratic nature of the Internet—that it is a massive, amorphous city-state of ever-changing information, sports scores, nut-job militia postings, e-mail between one-celled animals, and pornography, somehow run by everyone, someone, anyone, and no one at the same time. Not true. It was created in Nashville in 1963 by Vanderbilt University computer science professor George

Lindsay, well known to fans of *The Andy Griffith Show*. "The Net," Prof. Lindsay once said, "is what made Goober rich."

# What You Need to Use the Internet

- A computer.

- A nerd manservant with bad posture, poor eyesight, and no friends. It will be like having your personal Bill Gates.

- A modem that connects your computer to the Net. Internet junkies will tell you not to buy a modem with less than 28,800 bps, but really, the object here is to get maybe 1,200 bps or 2,400 bps at most. Yes, that will move you very, very slowly through cyberspace. But the trick here is that when you're ever so slowly downloading naked pictures of Aretha Franklin from the Rock 'n' Roll Hall of Fame Web site, you can also do your laundry.

# What Is a Web Site?

The Web stands for another part of Internet history. About fifteen years after Prof. Lindsay founded the Internet (and after his successful run on *Hee Haw*), he created the sitcom *Webster* with Emmanuel Lewis, Susan Clark, and Alex Karras. Goober named the World Wide Web(ster)— a region of information and graphics—as homage to Emmanuel. The *Webster* page remains the busiest site on the Web, receiving millions of "hits," or requests for information, on the life of Emmanuel Lewis every day.

# Home Sweet Home Page

When your mouse (gerbil or hamster) leads you onto the Web, you will start your visit to the many mostly useless sites with a home page. Anybody can have a site and, thus, a home page. Anybody. In his great wisdom, Goober allowed anybody with a computer and enough periods and slashes on his keyboard to design a place from which they could pollute cyberspace. Once you reach a home page, you can connect to various "links" to find your way to the trove of goodies waiting for you. A typical home page looks like this:

---

### WELCOME TO MY PERSONAL HOME PAGE

---

I am an inmate at San Quentin Prison.

I was recently incarcerated for decapitating three tourists from Holland who annoyed me when they did not use proper urinal etiquette.

My hobbies are needlepoint, whittling, and collecting classic lunchboxes featuring the characters of *The Brady Bunch*.

As the Death Row librarian and social director, I can recommend good books for you to read. Here are some of my favorite authors:

- <u>Jack Henry Abbott</u>

- <u>Caryl Chessman</u>

- <u>The Galloping Gourmet</u>

- <u>Al Franken</u>

- <u>Martha Stewart</u>

I am also on the lookout for Timmy the Tooth videos. They tell wonderful, wholesome stories, but they aren't available in the prison library. You can e-mail me at **buttboy@squent.bighouse.edu**.

---

Here's how to interpret the home page: Every boldfaced, underlined entry is one of zillions of links of available information. So if you plop your mouse on *The Brady Bunch*, you can access everything on the fictional family from the escort service run by Ann B. Davis to how Robert Reed became a transsexual on a two-part episode of *Medical Center.*

## *What Exactly Is E-Mail?*

The future of mankind. It will eliminate the Postal Service, fax machines, bicycle messengers, all overnight package deliverers, the telephone, and small talk. To be able to communicate by e-mail with people anywhere from 12 feet to 12,000 miles away is an advance on a par with Gutenberg's invention of the printing press.

Here is a typical look at an e-mail message: Thanks to a program called Endora—named while the founder was watching *Bewitched*—it gets flung to its recipient in cyberspace.

From hillary@westwing.whouse.gov
Wed Apr 19 10:38:30 1996
Return-Path: <hillary@westwing.whouse.gov>
To: bclinton@ovaloff.whouse.gov
Cc: socks@lawn.grass.gov
Subject: Press office

I'll be playing touch football with Sam Donaldson's toupee at 4:15 on the South Lawn. Kennedys will be there. So will Dole. We'll try to tear the ball out of his left hand.
Are you free?
—Hillary

## *Why Do They Write So Funny on the Net?*

Goober believed that to disguise his country upbringing, where his way of speaking was mocked, he had to create an obscure new language that looked real smart, but was as foreign to most people as rural Mayberry slang was to wiseguys from Bensonhurst. So, a link to the Web looks something like this:

**http://www.hooters.hefner.sex/xxx**

Or an e-mail address looks like this:

**unabom@montana.shack.org**

They make sense in their own odd ways, except for http and //. For the nerdiness-impaired, here are some explanations:

| sign | meaning | explanation |
|------|---------|-------------|
| http | high-tech trash pile | Helen Crump Aunt Bee told Goober |
| // | put two slashes here | Goober forgot why he didn't stop at one. |

## *Communication on the Net*

One of the keys to sending messages back and forth through the Net is to convey the nuances of what you're writing. After all, the recipients of your ransom e-mail can't see your expressions as you type in your inane little messages. So here are some symbolic faces to type in at appropriate spots to punctuate your missives. To interpret the icons, just tilt your head to the left:

| Face As Typed | Meaning |
|---------------|---------|
| (:-) | I'm a bald guy smiling. |
| (:-D | I'm a bald guy laughing. |
| (;-D | I'm a bald guy laughing and winking. |
| {I:-( | I'm a hairy guy with one eyebrow going across his face, frowning. |
| {— | The umbrellas of Cherbourg. |
| (:-X | My baldheaded lips are sealed. |

| | |
|---|---|
| (%-) | This bald guy's eyes are glazed over from being on Net for 48 hours. |
| #:-) | My name is Archie Andrews. |
| (:-# | Help, Archie's on my face. |
| }l-o | I have a comb-over. I am sleeping. |
| -(:-) | I'm a smiling Mohawk wearer. |

## *How to Say What You Mean on the Net*

**BS WARNING**

To the uninitiated, communicating on the Net is like talking Bantu to a koala bear. It just doesn't work. So you need to study on-line language before you even think of talking in NetSpeak to devoted get-a-lifers already sending crucial messages to each other about dinner reservations.

| | |
|---|---|
| <ns> | Not smiling |
| <cktph> | Can't keep talking, prostate hurts |
| GOOMW | Get out of my way |
| FAQ | Frequently Asked Questions to avoid asking so as not to look like a schmuck to frequent users. The FAQs can be accessed at news groups where information is exchanged. Typical FAQ: Why are you asking that? |
| FOS | Full of shit |
| GOOMC | Get offa my cloud |
| —{{{}}}— | When you see me give me big hugs. |
| <tush> | Totally useless stuff here |

# Chapter 13

# DRIVING FOR REAL DUMMIES

## Note: For Beginners Who Want to Learn How to Drive

Always bear in mind that operating a motor vehicle takes some serious, conscientious effort. Of course, for those who already know how to drive a car, the process seems so easy and care-free. However, for those who haven't yet learned, the first time behind the wheel can be a frightening and even terrifying experience.

## Dealing with All Those Jitters

Don't be embarrassed. Getting behind the steering wheel for the first few times can be a bit overwhelming. Here's a suggestion. Take a few deep breaths before you get in the car. Perhaps have a shot of scotch or bourbon to calm your nerves. Remember—safety first! We can't have any nervous drivers out on the roads!

## Making the Necessary Adjustments

Too many beginners simply want to get in the car, turn on the ignition, and roar out of the driveway. Not so fast. First you have to make certain that the motor vehicle has been specially adjusted to fit your personalized driving needs.

That means taking a few moments to check the radio to make certain all the music stations you want have been programmed properly. Check the volume as well as bass and treble levels.

Take another moment to make certain that the air-conditioning unit is already cranked up to its top level *before you start the car.* Otherwise, when you do turn the ignition, you might have to wait a few precious extra seconds before you're bathed in arctic air.

Most important, *check the rearview mirror* and make certain that it's properly placed (so that you can instantly check your hair and make certain that your sunglasses look good).

Finally, if you have some spare time, see whether your car has seat belts.

# Starting the Car

The car key is essential to this process. You simply place the key in the ignition switch and turn it. A few options are available here:

- If the engine guns, then you have succeeded in starting the car.

- If an awful screeching sound occurs, it's a good chance you're trying to start your car even though it's already running. We suggest that you stop trying to start a car that's already been started.

- If the awful screeching sounds continue to occur, you might want to check whether your cat was near the tires of the car when you started it.

## *Putting the Car into Operation*

You'll note on the gear shift that the car can normally only go in two directions—frontward or backward. On the shift, however, there are a number of letters. The only letters that should interest you are "D," for drive, and "R," for reverse. Drive means go forward. Reverse means go backward. The other letters on the gear shift (such as L, N, or S) are merely the initials of the individual who put together your car at the assembly plant.

## *Driving Your Car in Traffic*

For beginners, you'll find that once you get the car out on the road you'll be terrified by the thought of confronting oncoming traffic. To that end, try keeping the car to the RIGHT of the yellow line. This will definitely lessen the possibility of a head-on crash.

You might also want to consider taking your left foot off the brake pedal while your right foot is on the accelerator. Again, experienced drivers will tell you that it's difficult to gain much speed while you have one foot pressing down on the brake.

NOTE: It's never a good idea to open the car door while you're driving the car. Too many things can fall out when you do this, such as your CD's, beer cans, passengers, you, etc.

## *What the Various Traffic Lights Mean*

Simple. A RED light means you should come to a full stop.

A GREEN light means go.

A YELLOW light is the DMV's Challenge Round, in which you have to calculate instantaneously whether you should speed up to get through the intersection before the light turns red or hit the brakes and stop.

## *Always Take Your Car Keys with You!*

For some unknown reason, drivers always seem tempted to lock the car doors with the keys still in the ignition. This makes re-entry into the automobile extremely difficult and vexing. Nobody knows why so many people do this, but it's a common, everyday occurrence all over the world. Make a mental note NOT to do this.

Always keep an extra set of keys stashed in your glove box in the car, just in case you accidentally lock your keys in the car.

# Chapter 14

# TAXES FOR REAL DUMMIES

## *Why We Pay Taxes*

The vast majority of our tax dollars goes to subsidize the salaries of the Internal Revenue Service and their employees, and of course, to pay the full salaries and expenses of our Congressmen and Senators in Washington, DC.

## *Why You Should Pay Taxes...*

Good question.

## *What the IRS Can Do to You...*

Quite frankly, they'll throw you in jail for nonpayment of taxes. You'll have to grub it out every day with the likes of such hardened criminals as Pete Rose, Leona Helmsley, Michael Milken, and other celebrity types.

You'll be sentenced to do hard time in a minimum-security jail where you'll get three squares a day, a rent-free room, cable TV, air-conditioning, use of an exercise room, a full library, and lots of other federally mandated rights. Yes, you're right—it does sound like hell.

# How Not to Get Audited

What's the worst thing that can happen to you when it comes to doing your taxes? Being notified that the IRS would like to see you for a little chat...

To that end, here are a few quick tips on how to insure you *won't* get that note in the mail:

**Tip #1:** The messier your return, the less likely you are to be audited. Include lots of cross-outs and White-out. Who at the IRS wants to waste time going through a sloppy return?

**Tip #2:** If you aren't certain about precise numbers in your deductions, just estimate. But be careful never to use even numbers. For example, don't list travel and entertainment as merely $4,000, auto expenses as $2,000, and professional dues at $1,000; instead, go with "real" numbers like: $4,532.17, $2,349.11, and $1,289.90.

**Tip #3:** Receipts can be manufactured. In fact, be sure to purchase a copy of *Receipts for Real Dummies*, by DIG Publishing, and fill out accordingly.

# Filling Out the 1040 Form

How to fill out the form in easy instructions.

Gross adjusted income—Define each term individually: "gross" is meant to be a personal insult, as in, "You only made what? That's gross!" "Adjusted" is the IRS's way of suggesting that they already know you're cheating on your tax by "adjusting" your reported income. "Income" means just that—how much money you're openly admitting to having made.

Exemptions—Anybody (or anything) that sponges off your paycheck. This includes your kids, in-laws, your good-for-nothing brother who can't hold down a steady job, your ex-wife and, of course, all household pets (including the crows that chow down from your garbage cans once a week).

| Form **1040** | Department of the Treasury—Internal Revenue Service | **1995** | (99) | IRS Use Only—Do not write or staple i |
| U.S. Individual Income Tax Return | | | |

For the year Jan. 1–Dec. 31, 1995, or other tax year beginning , 1995, ending , 19 C

**Label**
(See instructions on page 11.)
**Use the IRS label.** Otherwise, please print or type.

| Your first name and initial | Last name | Your social : |
| If a joint return, spouse's first name and initial | Last name | Spouse's soc |
| Home address (number and street). If you have a P.O. box, see page 11. | Apt. no. | For Priva Paperwo Act Notic |
| City, town or post office, state, and ZIP code. If you have a foreign address, see page 11. | | |

**Presidential Election Campaign**
(See page 11.)

Do you want $3 to go to this fund? . . . . . . . . . Yes No
If a joint return, does your spouse want $3 to go to this fund? . . . .

**Filing Status**
(See page 11.)
Check only one box.

1 Single
2 Married filing joint return (even if only one had income)
3 Married filing separate return. Enter spouse's social security no. above and full name here. ▶
4 Head of household (with qualifying person). (See page 12.) If the qualifying person is a child but n enter this child's name here. ▶
5 Qualifying widow(er) with dependent child (year spouse died ▶ 19 ). (See page 12.)

**Exemptions**
(See page 12.)

6a **Yourself.** If your parent (or someone else) can claim you as a dependent on his or her tax return, **do not** check box 6a. But be sure to check the box on line 33b on page 2
b Spouse . . . . . . . . . . . . . . . . . . . . . . .
c Dependents: | (2) Dependent's social security number. If born | (3) Dependent's relationship to | (4) No. of months lived in your

# What Is Tax-Deductible?

Every year, there's much confusion about what you can legally deduct. Too many people try to find the answers in commercial tax guides, or by consulting with their accountants. The result? Lots of needless confusion.

Here's a better idea. Why not simply deduct everything you can, then let the IRS figure out what's legit and what isn't? Here's a list of deductible items to declare on your schedule C:

- 100% interest on mortgage payments, 100% on home equity loans, 100% on car loans, 100% on credit card interest. Most people don't seem to declare these easy-to-compute deductions.

- All travel-and-entertainment is 100% tax-deductible. Any gifts to friends, including Xmas presents to spouses, mistresses, children, friends, buddies, etc. Donations to charity, such as your church, are also 100% deductible. However, be certain to get a receipt from your minister whenever the plate is passed on Sunday.

Besides, taking a deduction for a home office is a great way to save money. You can deduct typical working expenses, such as electricity, heating, water, cable television, telephones, liquor, food, and just about everything else.

Also: In a landmark case in 1995, a woman who worked out of her home as a prostitute was allowed to claim her bedroom as a legal place of business as a home office (see *IRS* v. *Fleiss*).

P.S. to divorcees! Don't forget that alimony payments are also tax-deductible! (see *In Re Oscar Madison* v. *Blanche Madison*).

# Chapter 15

# PERSONAL FINANCE FOR REAL DUMMIES

## You're Not Dumb, You Just Have No Money

**What Is Money?**
Colored, printed paper and jingly metal. Money is good. The more you have, the happier you are. The less you have, the more likely you are to buy *The National Enquirer*.

## Knowing Your Money: How to Carry It and Fold It

Money is legal tender. TENDER. Soft. Easy to blush.

No matter how you receive money—whether it's folded, spindled, or mutilated—you must show it the proper respect by folding it nicely and neatly. Never write on it. Never leave it in your back pocket so your sweaty buttocks can make it wet and smelly.

**Tip:** Fold out all the dog-ears from each dollar bill and place it neatly in your wallet, with decreasing denominations going to the rear.

DENOMINATION means the value of each bill. $1, $2, and $10 are denominations.

## *Where You Should Carry Your Wallet*

**Men:** Placing it in your back pocket will remind you that it is always there because of the uncomfortable feeling you will have when you sit down.

**Women:** Place it in your purse or handbag along with the other essentials: lipstick, tweezers, nail polish, polish remover, tampon, and a photo of your first boyfriend dating back to 1978.

## *You're Planning to Save Your Pennies!*

To save your pennies in a neat way, get penny holders—small paper cylinders—from your bank. A holder accommodates fifty pennies. But sometimes the fit is tight and one or more pennies do not rest horizontally, which means you'll have to start over again. ESTIMATED TIME OF LOADING FOR THE INEXPERIENCED: three minutes.

Three undistinguished Presidents—Grant (Mudcat), Cleveland (Reggie) and McKinley (Mount)—somehow made their ways onto the $50, $500, and $1,000 bills. And Woodrow Wilson appears on the $100,000 bill, which no one but the Federal Reserve sees. If you happen to find one, mail it directly to us. We'll make sure it gets into the right hands. Or the left ones.

# Cash Is Not the Only Money There Is

### Telling Cash from Other Forms of Money

Cash has preprinted numbers on it. But when you have a CHECK, you can write in any numbers you want. A check is a piece of paper, usually arranged in a pad, that lets you pay others for what you want or what you owe.

In order to use checks, you must go to a bank and deposit real money. It can be cash. A check. Pennies. Gold pieces. Beads. Check writing is really a little game. Banks generally do not like you to write checks for more than the sum of money you have put in the bank. That's called an overdraft. It is bad. Unless you're a Congressman.

You may also have a CREDIT CARD. It is plastic and has numbers on it. The numbers are raised. It is a license to spend money. You can spend as much as you want until a snotty store clerk pulls a pair of scissors out and cuts it in half. Then you can't spend anymore. But wasn't that fun?

# Measuring Your Financial Health

Have you looked at your bank book lately? Does "overdrawn" mean anything to you? The great news is you can borrow at rates above 24 percent to finance what you owe, allowing you to boast of a new status symbol: a debt that you can never repay if you pay the minimum monthly payment.

Then you can borrow even more at a higher rate. The more you borrow at higher rates, the healthier the banks are. If the banks aren't healthy, they can't lend you money. If they can't lend money, they don't get payments, and they go out of business. This will lead to the economic ruin of the entire world! Just remember: Without you and your high-rate borrowing, Wall Street would collapse.

**Interest**
This means not only what you get paid from your bank
account, but what you pay when you borrow. In both cases,
you benefit from the highest rates. Banks, with their finely
tuned sense of fairness, will give you two to three percent
interest on your savings account and demand a modest 15.25
percent on a loan.

## How Can You Tell Good Credit from Bad Credit?

Who cares? The bottom line: The more you buy on credit,
the more you have. Ed Norton and Ralph Kramden made
the same salary, about $65 a week. Yet Norton had every
modern convenience in his Bensonhurst apartment, while
Ralph had a house that looked like Yucca Flats after
the blast.

Who was better off? Who was happier? Norton.

## What Are the Symbols of Your Credit Health?

**A Lot of Credit Cards:** Not just your average Discover and
American Express cards. But Visa and MasterCards from
every bank that will accept you and a bunch more issued
with sports teams, cartoon characters, and college names.

**An 18 Percent Mortgage:** You're an old-fashioned home-
owner and a terrific American to boot. Banks can go bankrupt on seven percent mortgages. Too many homeowners
have refinanced mortgages with high interest rates to those
with low ones. So remember: Bargain those rates up!

**Bankruptcy:** It no longer means you're a complete deadbeat!
Just a partial one. Many bankrupt people are permitted to

keep their cars, houses, and flatware while only having to give up some of their children and pets to pay their creditors. Bankruptcy can make you feel like a star—like Kim Basinger, Bernhard Goetz, or LaToya Jackson! Or a major company—like Continental Airlines! They've all gone into the financial toilet, flushed around and came back happy as people with a loanshark for a business partner.

In bankruptcy, you often get to rip off those whom you owe money because a judge lets you pay often as little as ten cents on every dollar you owe. Sometimes whole areas of debt can be eliminated, like your telephone bill, your rent, even your child support!

## *When Your Debt Load Is So High Even Publishers Clearinghouse Won't Give You Their Money*

Attractive and sophisticated as heavy interest payments are, they can sometimes get out of hand. Now is the time to seek professional help from a credit counselor or Big Debtors Anonymous, which has a simple nine-question test. If you answer "yes" to more than half the following questions, you may be a compulsive Debt Schmuck:

1. Do your debts have you so worried that you're missing nightly reruns of *The Simpsons*?

2. Are you feeling so pressured that it keeps you from remembering to steal other people's treats from the company refrigerator?

3. Do people wear cloves of garlic around you?

4. Are you giving the credit history of a cousin you dislike in order to get more credit cards?

5. Has the tension caused by your debt problems grown so large that you often forget you've left your son in the

car seat, or on the roof, of the new four-wheel-drive
vehicle you bought with counterfeit $100 bills from the
Middle East?

6. Have you tried to get drunk on nonalcoholic beer to
   forget that you can't even pay for your daughter's latest
   set of Pogs?

7. Have you taken to jotting down the names of recently
   deceased people from the obituary section of the news-
   paper so you'll have aliases with which to apply for more
   credit?

8. Do you eat and sleep in your new Mercedes, desperately
   filling out credit applications for cards like the CatChow
   Visa Card?

9. When you sleep, do you dream of Mr. Potter in *It's A
   Wonderful Life?*

## *The Truth About Stocks and Bonds*

The bottom line lies in their names: They restrict you.
Stocks were derived from the form of punishment in which
one's wrists and ankles were forcibly confined until you
handed over all your money to the town constable. Bonds
were derived from the ropes that the constable's wife used
to tie the constable to his Chippendale bed.

## *Balance Is a Key to Your Investment Future*

Sure, you can be a risk-taker. Buy one share in AT&T, one
Con Edison bond, one 1,000-year Treasury bill and track
their nutty one-to-two percent annual moodswings. But that
doesn't provide balance or fun. Here is how a conservative
investor with $10,000 should pursue his goals:

**BONDS Invest 50 percent of your portfolio here:**
**Bosnian High-Yield Municipals:** Sarajevo sewer triple-salchow munis, free of state, city, or federal taxation. Except in Croatia.

**Orange County Fantasyland Bonds:** Disney Eats Anaheim omnis, free of California, county, Anaheim, Mighty Duck, or Goofy taxes. Michigan Militia Tax-Frees: The militia doesn't believe in the IRS, monogamy, or proper dental hygiene. Purchase of these "MichMils" requires proof of gun ownership and ten years' residency in an NRA-approved compound.

**STOCKS: 20 percent**
**MGM Not-So Grand, Series B:** Small hotels, small airlines, small casinos, small employees who get small salaries.

**T.I.T.:** Entertainment conglomerate that is holding company for Playboy, Penthouse, and Hooters magazines. Owns the Wonder Bra and is a leading manufacturer of breast pumps.

**Chrystler:** Maker of the Popemobile, the Dalai LeMans and the Volkswagen Rabbi.

**MUTUAL FUNDS: 20 percent**
**T. Rowe Price Surgeon General Select:** Buys stocks and bonds of corporations that manufacture cigarettes, liquor, motorcycles, semi automatic assault rifles, nuclear power plants, and armor-piercing Black Talon bullets.

**Fidelity Infidelity:** Specializes in Motel 6, Hilton, Marriott Hotels, and other very-out-of-the-way motor inns.

**Merrill Lynch Eurotrash:** Invests in whatever Claus Von Bulow says you should. In the last quarter of 1996, Mr. B recommends a shift into leather and pharmaceutical manufacturers.

**VENTURE CAPITAL: 10 percent**
Minority share of a franchise in Michael Milken Junk Hair Club for Men franchise.

# GLOSSARY

An alphabetical listing of terms, complete with their meaning and usage.